Contents

Unit 1 Alphabetical Order
Alphabetical order, letters of the alphabet 1–4
Alphabetical order by first letter in words 5–7
Unit 1 Review 8

Unit 2 Nouns
Recognizing nouns 9–12
Plural nouns with -s 13–15
Unit 2 Review 16

Unit 3 Nouns and Verbs—Agreement
Nouns with verbs <u>is</u> and <u>are</u> 17–18
Using <u>am</u> with <u>I</u> 19
<u>Is, are, am</u> review 20
Verbs, -ing form 21–22
Plain form of verbs 23
Unit 3 Review 24

Unit 4 Verb Tenses
Past tense forms, adding -ed 25
Irregular past tense forms
    did 26
    came 27
    went 28
    saw 29
    review 30
    had 31
    gave, sat 32
    took, found 33
Unit 4 Review 34

Unit 5 Word Meanings
Antonyms
    first, last 35
    long, short; high, low 36
    on, off; over, under 37
    left, right 38
    top, bottom; before, after 39
Multiple meaning words 40–41
Unit 5 Review 42

Check Up Test Units 1–5 43–44

Unit 6 Sentence Structure

Statements and questions 45–46
Question words...47–48
Exclamations...49–50
Sentence punctuation...51
Unit 6 Review...52

Unit 7 Capitalization

Names of people 53
The word I 54
Names and I review...55
Months...56–59
Unit 7 Review...60

Unit 8 Using Writing Signals

Initials..61
Initials and titles..62
Abbreviations for days 63
Abbreviations for months 64
Abbreviations review 65
Comma between day and year 66
Comma in direct address...67
Contractions 68–69
Unit 8 Review...70

Unit 9 Writing Good Sentences

Complete sentences 71–72
Compound words..73–74
Using a, an...75
Writing sentences review 76
Using he, she, it...77
Using they, we 78
Writing sentences review 79
Unit 9 Review...80

Unit 10 Writing Good Stories and Letters

Sequence in a story..81–83
Unity in a story 84–86
Writing a letter 87–89
Unit 10 Review...90

Check Up Test...91–92

Level
B

Step by Step
Language Skills

 **Continental Press**
Elizabethtown, PA 17022

Illustrations: Harry Norcross
Photo Credits: **Corbis Inc.:** Cover, *children talking, girl writing*
PhotoDisc, Inc.: Cover, *child reading*

ISBN: 0-8454-9578-X
© 2003 The Continental Press, Inc.

ABC Review

These are the ABC's.

Aa	Bb	Cc	Dd	Ee	Ff
Gg	Hh	Ii	Jj	Kk	Ll
Mm	Nn	Oo	Pp	Qq	Rr
Ss	Tt	Uu	Vv	Ww	Xx
Yy	Zz				

Write the ABC's with capital letters.

Write the ABC's with lowercase letters.

Alphabet Review

ABC Order

ABC order is the order of letters in the alphabet.

A B C D E F G H I J K L M N O P Q R S T U V W X Y Z

Draw a line from dot to dot in ABC order.

ABC Order

A B C D E F G H I J K L M N O P Q R S T U V W X Y Z

A    Q _ _ _ _ _   V _ _ _ _ _

N _ _ _ _ _   D _ _ _ _ _   J _ _ _ _ _

G _ _ _ _ _   Y _ _ _ _ _   L _ _ _ _ _

 T   _ _ _ _ D   _ _ _ _ G

_ _ _ _ J   _ _ _ _ B   _ _ _ _ V

_ _ _ _ Y   _ _ _ _ Q   _ _ _ _ M

3   Alphabetical Order

ABC Order

ABC order is the order of letters in the alphabet.

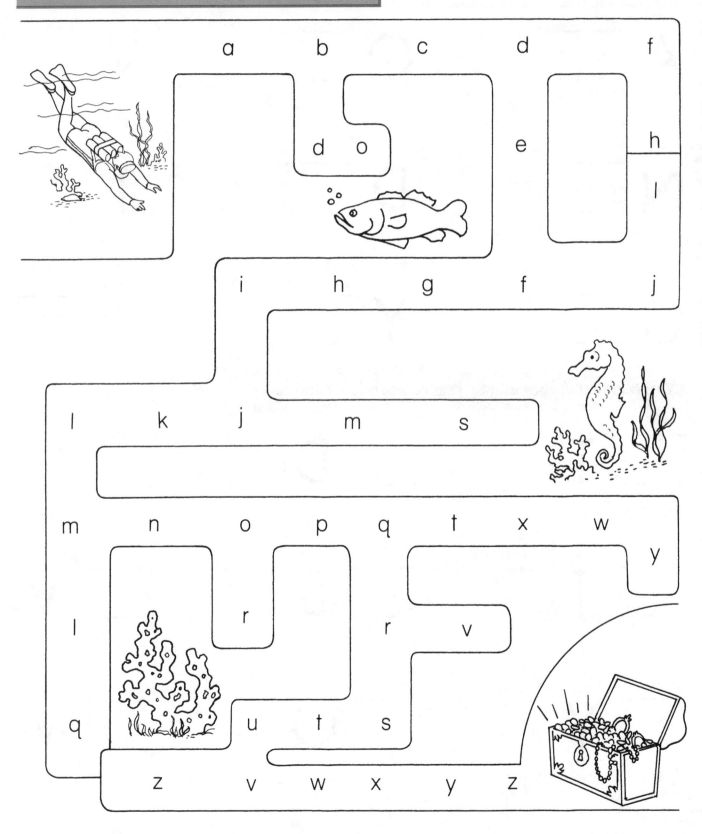

ABC Order

arm	fire	egg	car	ball	duck

Write each word from the box beside the letter it begins with.

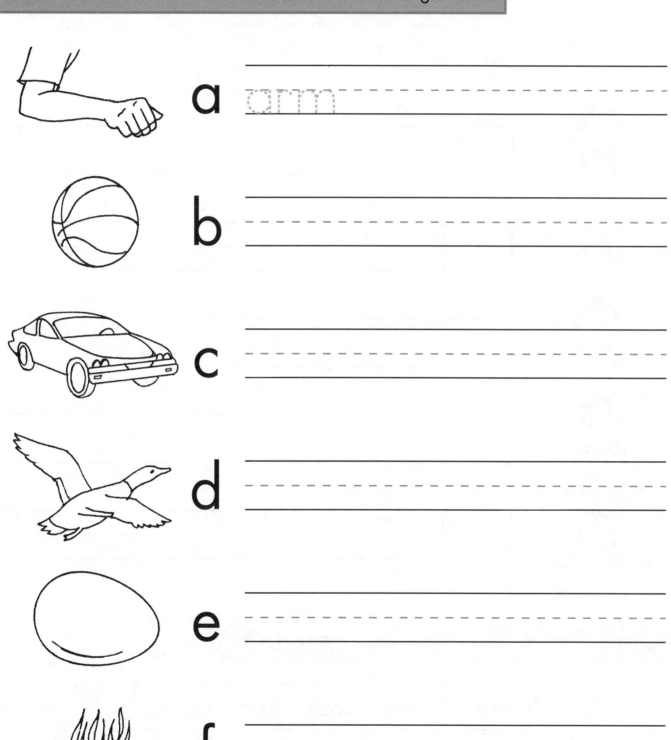

a   arm

b

c

d

e

f

ABC Order

ABC order is the order of letters in the alphabet.

Write these letters in ABC order in the boxes below.

| A | E | C | B | D |

A   Ana

[ ]

[ ]

[ ]

[ ]

Now write each of these names beside the letter it begins with.

| Ana | Carlos | Brad | Erin | Donna |

ABC Order

a b c d e f g h i j k l m n o p q r s t u v w x y z

Write the word for each picture. Then number the words in ABC order.

gate

1 gate

kite

leg

ice

hill

nine

jet

moon

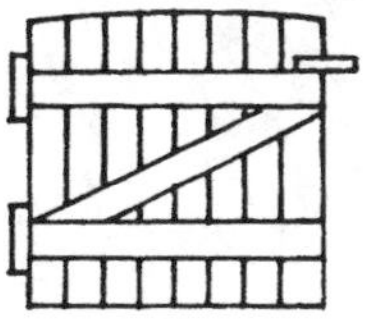

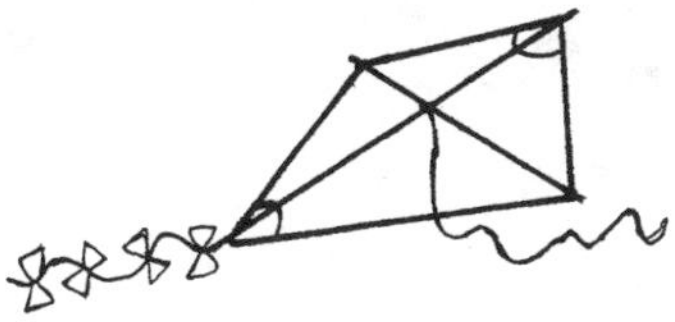

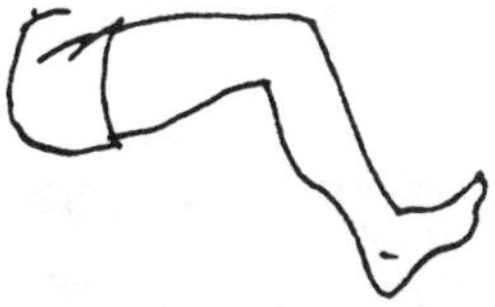

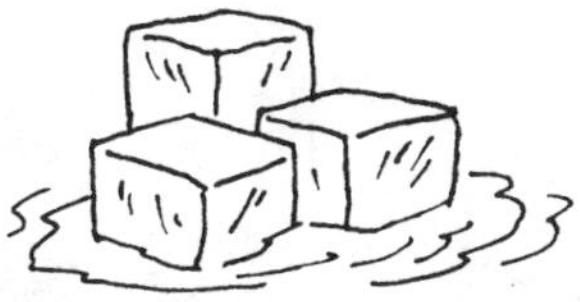

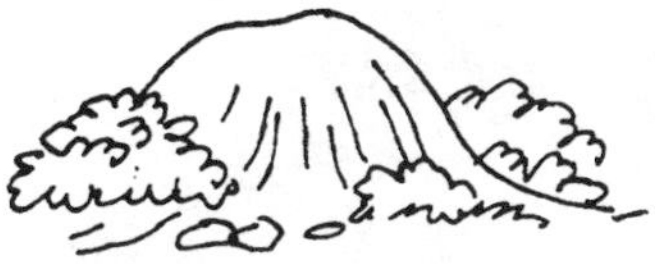

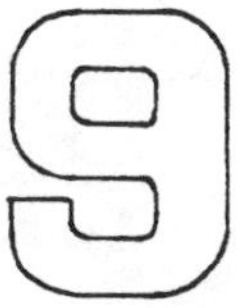

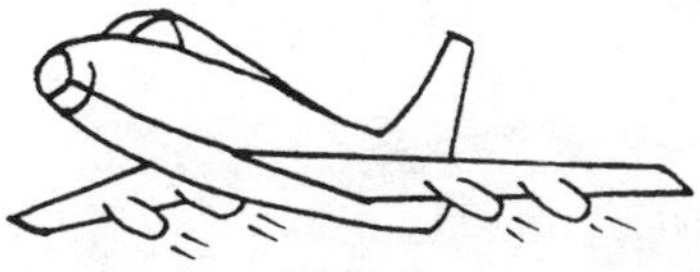

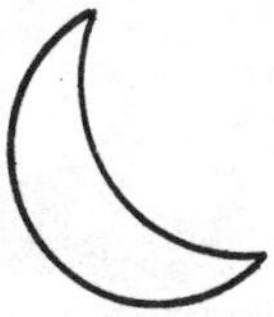

ABC Order

Number the words in ABC order.

_____ skate   _____ owl   _____ rain

_____ pig   _____ tree   _____ quilt

Write these letters in ABC order.

W   Z   U   Y   V   X

_____

- -

_____

Now write the lowercase letters that have the same names in ABC order.

_____

- -

_____

Nouns

Some words name people. These words are called **nouns.**

Draw a line from each word to the picture of the person it names.

boy •

doctor •

baby •

teacher •

girl •

cowboy •

9

Nouns

Some words name animals. These words are called nouns.

Put a <u>line</u> under the right name for each animal.

bear   bee

rabbit   cow

bee   dog

cow   horse

dog   bear

horse   rabbit

Put a (circle) around the picture each sentence tells about.

This is a bee.

That is a horse.

Here is a rabbit.

Nouns

Some words name things. These words are called nouns.

Write the number of each thing beside its name.

1.  2. 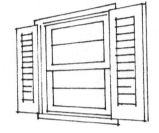 3.

4.  5.  6.

____ window   ____ bed   ____ shoe

____ hill   ____ cage   ____ truck

Put a (circle) around the picture each sentence tells about.

This is a bed.

Here is a shoe.

That is a truck.

Nouns

Nouns can name people, animals, and things.

Put a (circle) around the right noun.

1. A teacher / baby reads the book.

2. A foot goes in a coat / shoe.

3. A bed / book has a blanket.

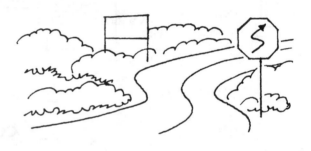

4. A boat / truck goes on a road.

5. Milk comes from a duck / cow.

6. A bird / bear has wings.

Nouns: More Than One

Nouns can name **one** and **more than one.**

bee

pans

cages

girl

birds

turtle

bags

barn

Write the nouns that name one.

Write the nouns that name more than one.

13

Nouns: More Than One

Nouns can name one and more than one.

boat

boat<u>s</u>

Write the nouns that name more than one.

truck _____

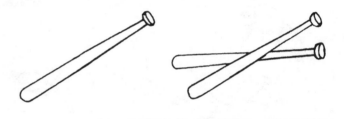

bat _____

bear _____

kitten _____

teacher _____

Nouns: More Than One

Nouns can name one and more than one.

Put a (circle) around the picture each sentence tells about.

1. This is a pig.

2. These are pens.

 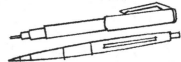

3. This is a balloon.

4. These are pears.

 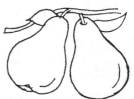

5. These are boys.

6. This is a book.

7. These are vans.

Plural Nouns with -s

Nouns

teacher   cake   fan   store   turtle   girl

teachers   cakes   fans   stores   turtles   girls

Write a word from the box to name each picture.

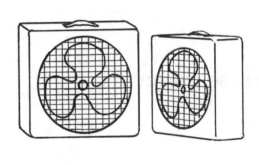

Nouns with Is, Are

Use **is** with nouns that tell about one.

Use **are** with nouns that tell about more than one.

A goat <u>is</u> a farm animal.

Ducks <u>are</u> farm animals, too.

Write **is** or **are** in each space to complete each sentence.

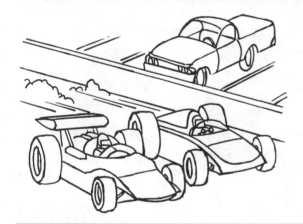

1. The cars _____ in a race.

2. The truck _____ not racing.

3. This party _____ fun.

4. The pizzas _____ ready.

5. This taco _____ good.

6. These chips _____ good, too.

Nouns and Verbs—Agreement

Nouns with Is, Are

Use **is** with nouns that tell about one.
Use **are** with nouns that tell about more than one.
Use **are** with two nouns joined by **and.**

Jamil <u>is</u> tall.
Colin and Omar <u>are</u> short.
The boys <u>are</u> friends.

Put a (circle) around the right word to use in each sentence.

1. Rosa and Nita is / are sisters.

2. Nita is / are by the window.

3. Rosa is / are beside Nita.

4. The airplanes is / are very big.

5. Nita and Rosa is / are ready to go.

6. The girls is / are going home.

Nouns and Verbs—Agreement

18

Using Am with I

Use **am** with **I.**

Write **am** to complete the sentences.

I <u>am</u> Pedro Díaz.

Today I _____ an actor.

In the play I _____ a king.

I _____ Leena Das.

I _____ a princess in the play.

In the story I _____ very pretty.

Write two things about yourself. Use the word **am.**

I am _____

I _____

Nouns and Verbs—Agreement

Nouns with Is, Are, Am

Write **is, are,** or **am** to complete the sentences.

Clowns _____ funny.

My jacket _____ new.

The pans _____ hot.

The money _____ here.

Put a (circle) around the right word in each sentence.

is
The zoo are down the street.
am

is
Many animals are there.
am

is
I are there every Monday.
am

Verbs

Some words tell about doing something. They are called **verbs.**

| reading laughing singing flying walking |

Write a verb from the box to complete each sentence.

1. This man is _____ .

2. Two birds are _____ .

3. Mrs. Day is _____ .

4. The boy is _____ .

5. Sara and Amanda are _____ .

Verbs, -ing Form

Verbs

Make sentences to tell about the picture.
Draw a line from the noun word box to the verb word box.

The girls	is flying.
The plane	are laughing.
I	are walking.
The bird	am reading.
The dogs	is singing.

Verbs

fly	walk	read	sit	play	sing

Write a verb from the box to complete each sentence.

1. We _____ books.

2. We _____ on chairs.

3. People _____ games.

4. I _____ on the sidewalk.

5. We _____ songs.

6. Children _____ kites.

23

Verbs—Plain Form

Nouns and Verbs

Write words from each box to tell about the pictures. The first one shows you how.

I	is playing.
Ed and Al	am a doctor.
The boy	are walking.
The girls	fly.
Bees	are boys.

The girls are walking.

Adding -ed

Verbs change to tell about the past. Many verbs add **-ed.**

look + ed → looked   Maria look<u>ed</u> at the TV.

Make the words in the box tell about the past.
Then write the **-ed** words in the sentences.

fix	ask	open	wait	call

1. Maria _____asked_____ her dad to help.

2. Dad _____ on the phone.

3. They _____ for a long time.

4. Dad _____ the door.

5. The man _____ the TV.

Past Tense Verbs

Did

Verbs change to tell about the past. Use **did** to tell about the past.

do → did

Complete the sentences.

1. Can Ali do it?

He _____ it!

2. Someone must do the dishes.

Gita _____ them.

3. Who will do a painting?

Lee _____ one.

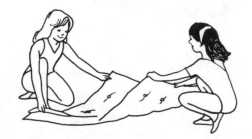

4. The girls want to do a trick.

They _____ it!

Came

Verbs change to tell about the past. Use **came** to tell about the past.

come → came

| Complete the sentences. |

1. Yoko _____ from Japan.

2. Manu _____ from India.

3. Juan _____ from Mexico.

4. Mara _____ from South Africa.

5. Luz _____ from Costa Rica.

6. Hamid _____ from Egypt.

27

Went

Verbs change to tell about the past. Use **went** to tell about the past.

go → went

Put a (circle) around the form of the verb that tells about the past.

1. Mom go / went to the store.

2. Eva went / go fishing.

3. Mai went / go to school.

4. Dad go / went to work.

5. Colin went / go to the mall.

6. Justin go / went to the park.

7. Peter go / went to the doctor.

8. His mother go / went with him.

Saw

Verbs change to tell about the past. Use **saw** to tell about the past.

see → saw

Write sentences to tell what Jenna saw at the farm.

Jenna saw a bird .

Jenna a .

Jenna a .

Jenna a .

Jenna a .

Past Tense Verbs

Did, Came, Went, Saw

Put a (circle) around each verb that tells about the past.

1. We did / do something new after school.

2. Marco and I go / went to the park.

3. Leila came / come , too.

4. Leila and I saw / see a rabbit.

5. Then we come / came to a pond.

6. Marco see / saw a turtle.

7. Later, we went / go home.

8. That night we do / did our homework.

Had

Verbs change to tell about the past. Use **had** to tell about the past.

have → had

Complete the sentences.

Before, Nick and Ryan _____ two tools.

They got one more tool.

Now they _____ three.

___

Before, I _____ one fish.

I got one more fish.

Now I _____ two.

___

Before, Inés and Kate _____ five combs.

They lost one comb.

Now they _____ four.

Gave, Sat

Verbs change to tell about the past.

give → gave

sit → sat

Put a (circle) around the verb that makes each sentence tell about the past.

1. What did you get for your birthday?

   Jake $\frac{\text{give}}{\text{gave}}$ me a game.

2. Did Mom have any money?

   She $\frac{\text{gave}}{\text{give}}$ Paco a dime.

3. Who gave the baby a toy?

   I $\frac{\text{give}}{\text{gave}}$ her that one.

4. Are these your books?

   Dad $\frac{\text{give}}{\text{gave}}$ them to me.

5. Who sat on my coat?

   The dog $\frac{\text{sit}}{\text{sat}}$ on it.

6. Did Jay ride the horse?

   He just $\frac{\text{sat}}{\text{sit}}$ on it.

7. Why is this chair here?

   Teresa $\frac{\text{sat}}{\text{sit}}$ on it.

8. Where did the cat go?

   The cat $\frac{\text{sat}}{\text{sit}}$ on the bed.

Took, Found

Verbs change to tell about the past.

take → took   find → found

Put a box around each verb that tells about the past.

1. Dad ᵗᵃᵏᵉ/took Jordan to the game.

2. They ᶠⁱⁿᵈ/found their seats.

3. Jordan ᵗᵒᵒᵏ/take off his cap.

4. Dad ᶠᵒᵘⁿᵈ/find the snack stand.

5. He ᵗᵒᵒᵏ/take some food to Jordan.

6. Their team ᵗᵃᵏᵉ/took the lead and won!

7. After the game they ᶠⁱⁿᵈ/found the bus stop.

8. They ᵗᵒᵒᵏ/take the bus home.

Past Tense Verbs

Past Tense Verbs

went   took   waited   sat
had   saw   did   asked
opened   gave   came   found

Change the verbs to tell about the past.
Look at the words in the box if you need help.

see _____

do _____

sit _____

have _____

take _____

come _____

find _____

open _____

go _____

give _____

ask _____

wait _____

Opposites

Words can tell something about people, animals, and things.
Some words, like **first** and **last,** are **opposites.**

Write **first** or **last** to complete each sentence.

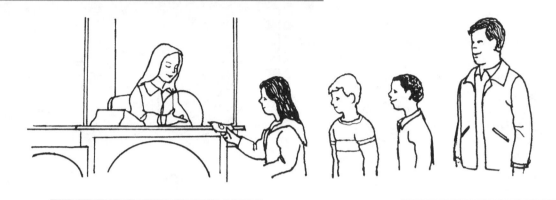

The girl is _____. The man is _____.

Put a <u>line</u> under the **first** person or animal in each picture.
Put a (circle) around the **last** person or animal.

35

Opposites

Words can tell something about people, animals, and things.
Some words are opposite in meaning.

Write **long** or **short** to tell about each thing.

long   short

One log is _____ .

The other log is _____ .

long   short

One train is _____ .

The other train is _____ .

Write **high** or **low** to tell about each thing.

This is a _____ mountain.

This is a _____ hill.

Opposites

Some words are opposite in meaning.

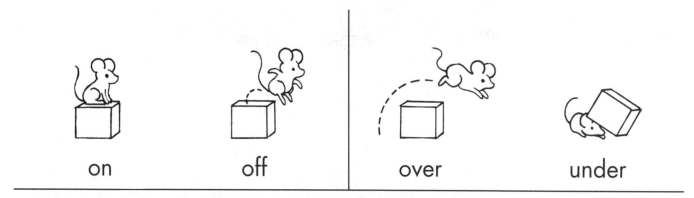

on   off   over   under

Draw a line from each picture and word to its opposite.

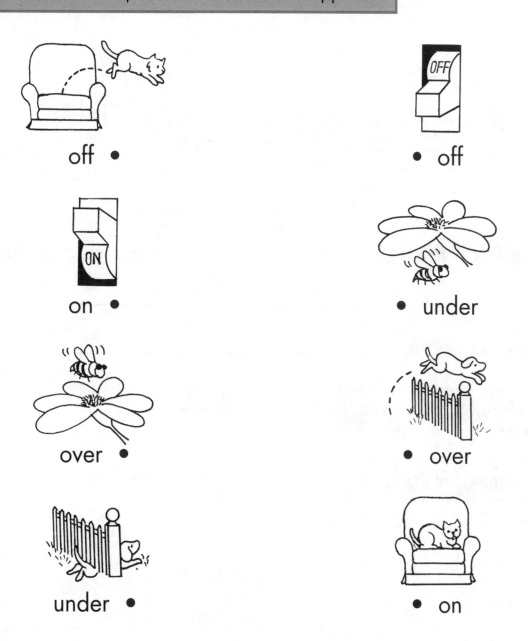

off •

• off

on •

• under

over •

• over

under •

• on

37

Opposites

Some words are opposite in meaning.

left  right

Write **left** or **right** to complete each sentence.

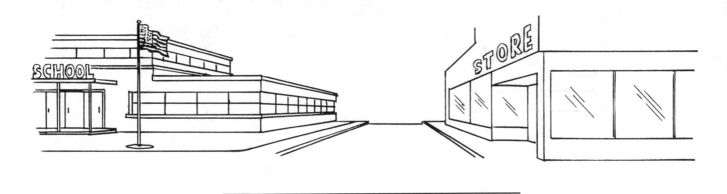

The store is on the _____ side of the street.

The school is on the _____ side.

Draw an arrow that points left. _____

Draw an arrow that points right. _____

Opposites

Some words are opposite in meaning.

Write the correct word in each space.

top

bottom

_____

- - - - - - - - - - - - - - - - - - - -

_____

_____

Put a (circle) around the person or thing on the **bottom.**
Put an X over the person or thing on **top.**

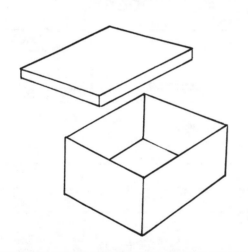

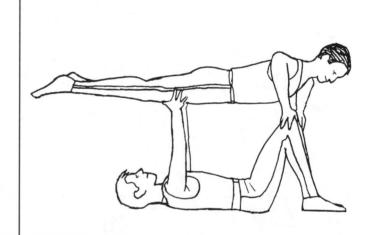

Write **before** or **after** to tell about the numbers.

1   2   3   4   5   6   7   8   9

2 comes _____ 3. | 7 comes _____ 8.

5 comes _____ 4. | 8 comes _____ 9.

Antonyms

Words with More Than One Meaning

A word can have more than one meaning.

nail   nail

Write a word from the box below each picture.
You will use each word two times.

bat	letter	pen

_____   _____
- - - - - - - - - -   - - - - - - - - - -
_____   _____

_____   _____
- - - - - - - - - -   - - - - - - - - - -
_____   _____

Words with More Than One Meaning

A word can have more than one meaning.

fish

fish

Write a word from the box to complete each sentence.
You will use each word two times.

fall	play	park

1. Some birds fly away in the _____.

2. Tim and I ride bikes in the _____.

3. Can you come out and _____ with me?

4. I will be a king in the school _____.

5. Walk slowly or you will _____.

6. Where did Dad _____ the car?

Multiple Meaning Words

Word Meanings

Draw a line from each word to its opposite.

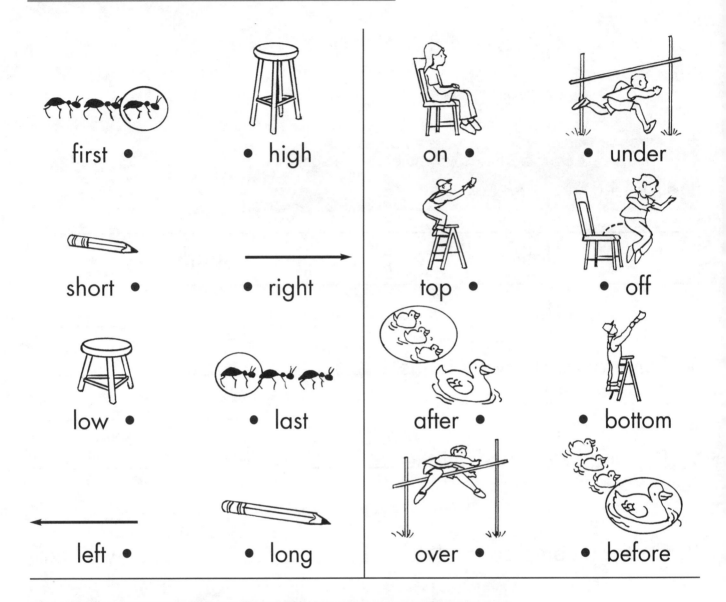

first •   • high

short •   • right

low •   • last

left •   • long

on •   • under

top •   • off

after •   • bottom

over •   • before

In each sentence, put a (circle) around the two words that are the same but mean different things.

Draw a line from each picture to the word it tells about.

1. I saw a man with a saw.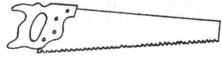

2. Yasmin likes to swing on a swing.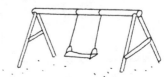

Check Up: Words

Circle the correct word or words in each sentence.

My name is Rita. I are watching a show. Dad and Mom is
           are   am   are

with me. We see a funny clown . He has four dog . The dogs is
                         clowns   dogs   are

doing tricks. The little white dog is off a high chair. The black
                                       on   low

dog is at the top of the ladder. Wags and Spot is sitting on
               bottom   are sitting

boxes. Wags has a long tail. Spot is the last dog. Spot will jump
                   short   first

through the hoop after Wags.
                  before

Check Up: Words

Clara	Kate	Olga	Zoe
Victor	Adam	Shane	Hugo

1. _____ 5. _____

2. _____ 6. _____

3. _____ 7. _____

4. _____ 8. _____

Put a (circle) around the verb that tells about the past in each sentence.

Bina and Sunil walk / walked home from school. Their dog came / come to

meet them. Sunil see / saw something shiny in the grass. He went / go to

look at it. He find / found a dime! Sunil already had / have two dimes. Bina

do / did not have any, so he give / gave the dime to her.

Sentences

All sentences begin with a capital letter.

- A sentence can tell.
  Jon is coming with us.

- A sentence can ask.
  Is Ben coming, too?

Cross out each small letter that should be a capital letter.
Write the capital letter above it.
Put a (circle) around **tells** or **asks** for each sentence.

1. this is Malik.   (tells)   asks

2. who is he calling?   tells   asks

3. he wants to talk to Tyler.   tells   asks

4. is Rosa on a train?   tells   asks

5. she likes to travel.   tells   asks

6. where will she go?   tells   asks

7. can you find the ball?   tells   asks

8. it must be here.   tells   asks

9. i saw it fall.   tells   asks

Kinds of Sentences

Sentences

All sentences begin with a capital letter.

<u>A</u> bee can fly

- A telling sentence is a **statement.**

It ends with a period.

<u>C</u>an a bear fly ?

- An asking sentence is a **question.**

It ends with a question mark.

Write the sentences correctly.

Begin all the sentences with a capital letter.

End the statements with a period.

End the questions with a question mark.

1. megan lives on a farm

_____

- -

_____

2. is it far from town

_____

- -

_____

3. her father has cows

_____

- -

_____

4. she has a pet rabbit

_____

- -

_____

5. are there many ducks

_____

- -

_____

Question Words: Who, What

Some questions start with a question word.

- **Who** asks about people.

Who is it?

- **What** asks about animals and things.

What is it?

Put a circle around the right question word to start each sentence. End each question with a question mark.

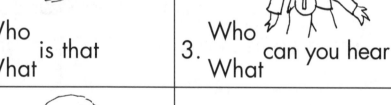

1. Who What is crying ?

2. Who What is that

3. Who What can you hear

4. Who What lives here

5. Who What laughed

6. Who What do you have

7. Who What can read

8. Who What is missing

9. Who What walked here

Question Words and Punctuation

Question Words: Where, When

Some questions start with a question word.

- **Where** asks about places.

Where is the bed?
It is near the window.

- **When** asks about time.

When do you go to school?
I go in the morning.

Write **Where** or **When** to start each question.
Use the statements to help you choose.
Be sure to begin all the sentences with a capital letter.

1. _____ is the dress?
   The dress is in a box.

2. _____ will it rain?
   It will rain tomorrow.

3. _____ do you sleep?
   I sleep at night.

4. _____ is that store?
   That store is on this street.

5. _____ is Tim going?
   Tim is going soon.

6. _____ is the money?
   The money is in my pocket.

7. _____ are the fish?
   The fish are in the water.

8. _____ does Jill paint?
   Jill paints after work.

Sentences

A sentence can show surprise or excitement.

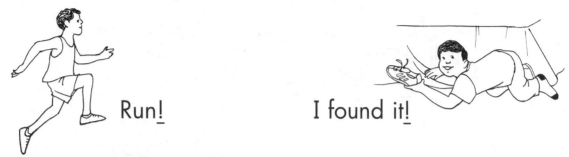

Run<u>!</u>

I found it<u>!</u>

End a sentence with this mark **!** to show surprise or excitement.

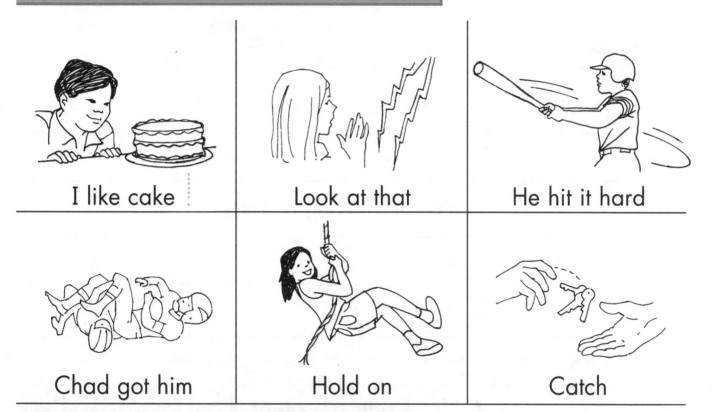

| I like cake | Look at that | He hit it hard |
| Chad got him | Hold on | Catch |

Circle the sentence you think the boy is saying.

Hurry!

Guess what I have!

Sentences—Exclamations

Sentences

A sentence that shows surprise or excitement ends with this mark **!**

It's a surprise<u>!</u>

Write these sentences. Make them show surprise or excitement.

1. Don't tell anyone

_____

2. We are having a party

_____

3. What a treat

_____

4. These gifts are great

_____

5. I am so happy

_____

Sentences

1. The grass is long

2. It needs to be cut

3. Trevor will do it

4. Aisha can help him

1. What time is it

2. Can we go soon

3. When will you be ready

4. Where is Jun

1. My truck is gone

2. I know it was here

3. I must find it

4. I think I see it

Sentences—Punctuation

Sentences

Cross out each letter that should be a capital. Write the capital letter above it. Use the right mark at the end of each sentence.

1. the boy is building something

2. he worked on it all morning

Write a sentence that tells what the boy is making.

_____

- -

_____

3. where do people sleep

4. is this a bed for a dog

Write a question about a picture on this page.

_____

- -

_____

5. watch out

6. do not sit on the bee

Write a sentence that shows surprise or excitement.

_____

- -

_____

Capital Letters: Names of People

Names of people begin with capital letters.

Jason Horn

Bibi Cook

Kelli Good

Ross Hand

Write the names of the people above to complete the sentences.

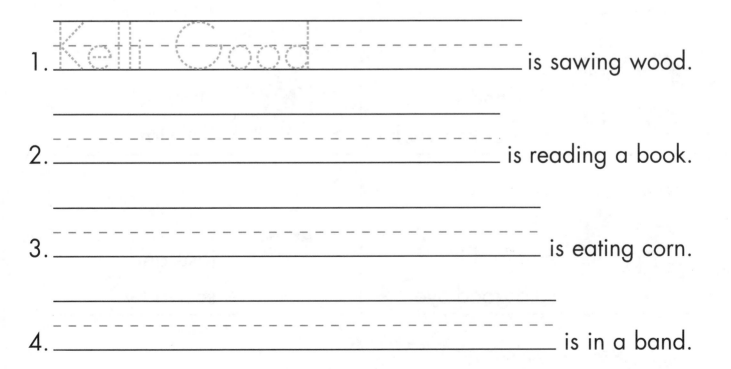

1. Kelli Good _____ is sawing wood.

2. _____ is reading a book.

3. _____ is eating corn.

4. _____ is in a band.

Capitalization—Names of People

Capital Letters: I

The word **I** is a capital letter. Names of people begin with a capital letter.

- When you name another person and yourself, you should name yourself last.

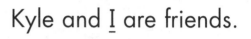

Kyle and I are friends.

Draw a line through each letter that should be a capital. Write the capital letter above it.

dara and i
made a pie.

blair and i
found a tie.

alex and i
did not know why.

cho and i
will stay dry.

erin and i
said good-bye.

josé and i
saw a fly.

Capital Letters

Sentences, names of people, and the word **I** begin with capital letters.

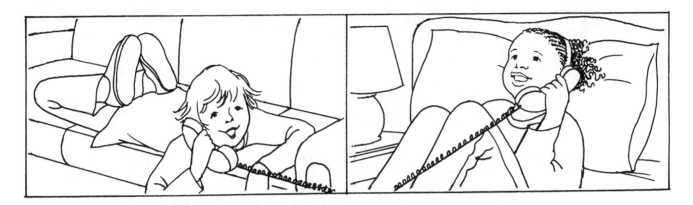

Draw a line through each letter that should be a capital.
Write the capital letter above it.

1. keesha brown and i are having a party. can you help us?

2. i would like to help. who can come to the party?

3. ahmed can come. he will bring mei lan with him.

4. can ana perez come? she makes good tacos.

5. ana and ramón can come. everyone will bring food.

6. nikki and i will bring ice cream. this party will be fun!

Capitalization—Review

Capital Letters: Months

Names of months begin with capital letters.

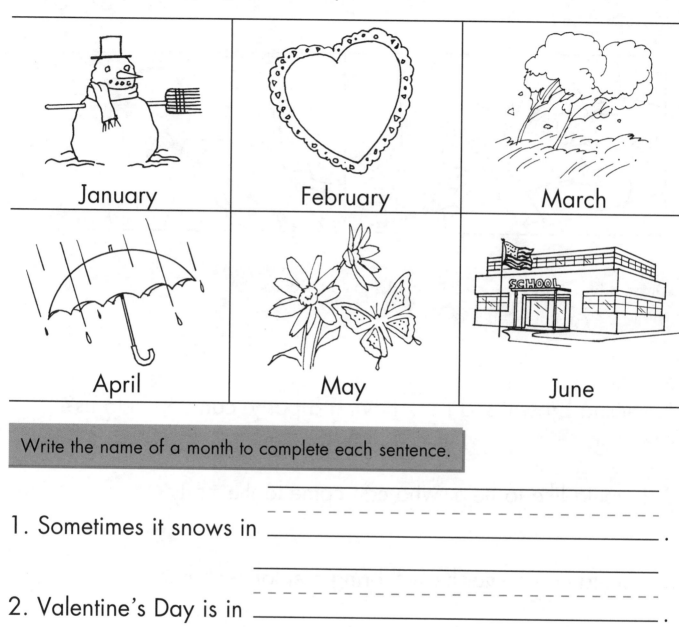

| January | February | March |
| April | May | June |

Write the name of a month to complete each sentence.

1. Sometimes it snows in _____ .

2. Valentine's Day is in _____ .

3. The wind blows in _____ .

4. It rains in _____ , and flowers come in _____ .

5. Some schools close in _____ .

Capital Letters: Months

Names of months begin with capital letters.

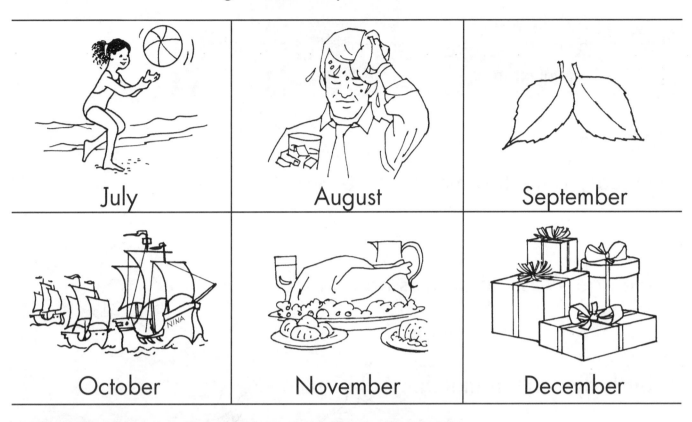

July	August	September

October	November	December

Write the name of a month to complete each sentence.

1. It is hot in _____ and _____ .

2. Fall begins in _____ .

3. Columbus Day is in _____ .

4. Thanksgiving Day is in _____ .

5. People give gifts in _____ .

Capital Letters: Months

Names of months begin with capital letters.

Draw a line through each letter that should be a capital letter.
Write the capital letter above it.

J
1. january is the first month of the year.

2. George Washington was born in february.

3. Birds fly north in march.

4. Some people play tricks on the first day of april.

5. Mother's Day comes in may.

6. june brings the first day of summer.

Write the name of the month that begins with F.

_____

- -

_____

Capital Letters: Months

Names of months begin with capital letters.

1. Independence Day is on july 4.

2. Davy Crockett was born in august.

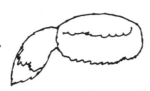

3. The first day of fall comes in september.

4. Some people play football in october.

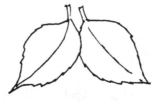

5. november can be a cold month.

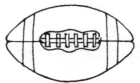

6. december is the last month of the year.

Write the name of the month your birthday is in.

_____

- -

_____

Capital Letters

Draw a line through each letter that should be a capital letter. Write the capital letter above it.

1. i bring people their newspapers.

2. sometimes julia vargas helps.

3. one paper is for yoshi sato.

4. victor and berta lópez get a paper, too.

Write the names of these months correctly.

january _____

march _____

august _____

Initials

An **initial** is the first letter of a name.
A period comes after an initial.

Tam Ho is <u>T.</u> Ho or <u>T.</u> <u>H.</u>
Joy Ann Talbert is Joy <u>A.</u> Talbert or <u>J.</u> <u>A.</u> Talbert or <u>J.A.T.</u>

Write these names.
Use an initial for the underlined names.

1. <u>Greg</u> Long

G. Long

2. Ana <u>Laura</u> Barrios

3. <u>Vijay</u> <u>Sarma</u>

4. <u>Amber</u> <u>Sue</u> Hill

5. <u>Marty</u> <u>Kay</u> <u>Jones</u>

6. <u>Dave</u> King

Writing Signals—Initials

Initials and Titles

An initial is a short way to write a name.
A period is used after an initial.

Mark Alan Black = Mark A. Black = M. A. Black = M.A.B.

A **title** often comes before a person's name.
A period is used after the title.

Dr.   Mr.   Mrs.   Ms.

Put a (circle) around each initial and each title in the sentences below.
Put a period after each initial or title.

1. This is Dr. G Bose.

2. He met Mr A T Rider.

3. Ms Rider is there, too.

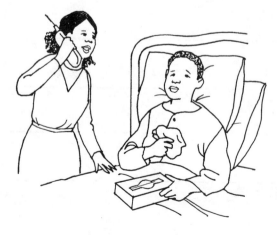

4. Mr C Jackson is not well.

5. Mrs Jackson is helping him.

6. She is calling Dr Lola E Alvarez.

Abbreviations: Days

An **abbreviation** is a short way to write a word.
- A period comes after an abbreviation.
- These are abbreviations for the names of the days of the week.

Sun.—Sunday   Tues.—Tuesday   Fri.—Friday

Mon.—Monday   Wed.—Wednesday   Sat.—Saturday

Thurs.—Thursday

Write the abbreviation for the name of the day that correctly answers each question.

1. Which day is the first day of the week? Sun.

2. Which day comes after Tuesday?

3. Which day begins the school week?

4. Which day comes before Friday?

5. Which day is the last day of the week?

Abbreviations: Months

A period comes after an abbreviation.
These are abbreviations for names of some months.

Jan—January   Apr—April   Oct—October

Feb—February   Aug—August   Nov—November

Mar—March   Sept—September   Dec—December

There are no abbreviations for **May, June,** or **July.**

Oct.

Feb.

Dec.

Sept.

Mar.

Jan.

Nov.

Labor Day

Thanksgiving

St. Patrick's Day

Columbus Day

Valentine's Day

Martin Luther King, Jr., Day

Christmas

Abbreviations

Draw a line from the name of each month to its abbreviation.

January	Mar.
February	Jan.
March	Apr.
April	Feb.
August	Sept.
September	Nov.
October	Aug.
November	Dec.
December	Oct.

Put a (circle) around the names of the months that have no abbreviations.

May	March	June
August	July	April

Write the abbreviations for the days named below.

Monday _____

Wednesday _____

Thursday _____

Saturday _____

65   Writing Signals—Abbreviations

Commas

A **comma** comes between the day and the year in a date.

December 5, 1943   May 1, 1892   June 18, 2000

Put a comma between the day and the year in each date below.

July 22, 1911   September 9 1952

August 12 1803   January 4 1945

November 6 1957   October 29 2001

Write the dates below correctly.
Put a period after each abbreviation.
Put a comma between the day and the year.

 Feb 12 1809 _____

 Mar 17 1922 _____

 Oct 21 1879 _____

Commas

A comma comes before or after the name of the person you are speaking to.

Put a <u>line</u> under the name of the person spoken to in each sentence.
Put a (circle) around the comma that comes before or after each name.

<u>Veda</u> , here is
the cage.

Thank you , Pran.

Salim , will you
play ball?

I want to
read now , Ama.

Ethan , come
with me.

I have to
work , Zach.

Lucía , what
is that?

This is my
new hat , Amy.

Contractions

A **contraction** is a word made from two words.
One or more letters are left out of the contraction.
An **apostrophe** takes the place of the missing letters.

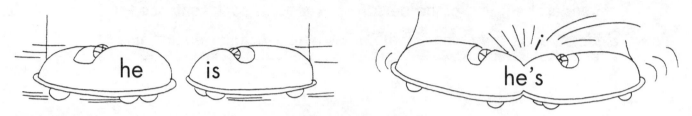

Make these words contractions.
Take out the **i** in **is.** Put an apostrophe in its place.

1. she is _she's_

2. it is _____

3. that is _____

4. there is _____

5. here is _____

6. he is _____

Contractions

A contraction is a word made from two words.
One or more letters are left out of the contraction.
An apostrophe takes the place of the missing letters.

they   +   will   =   ~~wi~~ they'll

> Write a contraction for the words under each line.
> Take out the **wi** in **will.** Put an apostrophe in its place.

1. ~~You'll~~ _____ have to hurry.
   You will

4. _____ bring the books.
   She will

2. _____ get the car.
   I will

5. _____ find his coat.
   He will

3. _____ go right away.
   We will

6. _____ wait for us.
   They will

69

Writing Signals

Write these names. Use initials for the underlined names.

Whitney Hayes _____

_____

Jade Lam Tang _____

Write the abbreviations for these words.

Doctor _____

Friday _____

Tuesday _____

January _____

Put a (circle) around the right contraction for each pair of words.

1. that is <   that's
            here's

3. she will <   she'll
                she's

2. they will <   there's
                 they'll

4. it is <   I'll
             it's

Write today's day and date. Use an abbreviation and a comma.

_____

_____

Sentences

Sentences have nouns and verbs.

- This is a sentence.
  It has a noun and a verb.   Fish swim.

- This is not a sentence.
  It does not have a noun.   Swimming fast.

- This is not a sentence.
  It does not have a verb.   Pretty fish.

Put a (circle) around each sentence.
Draw a line through the words that are not sentences.

1. The sun shines.
   ~~Sunny day.~~

2. The cow.
   Cows eat.

3. Birds fly.
   In the sky.

4. Rabbits hop.
   Hop and jump.

5. Brown horses.
   Horses run.

6. Trees grow.
   Green trees.

Sentences

Sentences have nouns and verbs.
Sentences begin with a capital letter and have a mark at the end.

- This is a sentence.

    The bus stops here.
- This is not a sentence.

    stops here on time

Draw a line through the words that are not sentences.
Make each sentence start with a capital letter and end with a period.

1. Here is a letter.
   a letter for you

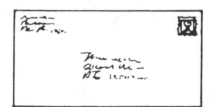

2. the pretty bird
   this bird talks

3. we watch TV
   the TV show

Write a sentence that tells about your pets.

_____

_ _ _ _ _ _ _ _ _ _ _ _ _ _ _ _ _

_____

Compound Words

A **compound word** is made up of two words.
The words are joined to make a new word.

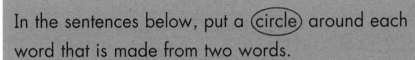

run + way = runway

In the sentences below, put a (circle) around each
word that is made from two words.
Draw a line to show where the words are joined.

1. Put these letters in the mailbox

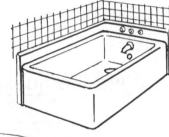

2. There is no water in the bathtub.

3. Where is your football?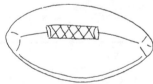

4. I have a cupcake.

5. Did Jan see the waterfall?

Word Building—Compound Words

Compound Words

A compound word is made up of two words.

Use the underlined words to make a compound word.
Write each new word beside the picture it names.

1. A <u>fish</u> that looks like a <u>cat</u> is a

_____

- -

_____

2. The <u>day</u> of your <u>birth</u> is your

_____

- -

_____

3. <u>Work</u> around the <u>house</u> is called

_____

- -

_____

4. <u>Books</u> for <u>school</u> are called

_____

- -

_____

5. A <u>place</u> for a <u>fire</u> is a

_____

- -

_____

Using A, An

Use **a** before words that begin with a consonant sound.
Use **an** before words that begin with a vowel sound.

 <u>a</u> <u>b</u>ag   <u>an</u> <u>a</u>nimal

Write **a** or **an** to complete each sentence.

1. Can _____ apple be green?

2. I put _____ egg in the cake.

3. We went on _____ picnic.

4. Do you have _____ ice cube?

5. Ted heard _____ owl last night.

6. Horses live in _____ barn.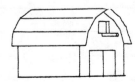

Word Usage—A, An

Writing Sentences

haircut	airplane	rainbow
cowboy	birdhouse	sunset

Write two sentences. Use compound words. You may use words from the box.

_____

- -

_____

_____

- -

_____

Write three sentences about this picture. Use **a** or **an** in your sentences.

_____

- -

_____

_____

- -

_____

Using He, She, It

The words **he, she,** and **it** can take the place of nouns and names.

Brandon reads well.   He reads many books.
Vanessa can ride.   She has a new bike.
A pony is little.   It gives rides to children.

Write **he, she,** or **it** to complete each sentence.
Remember to start each sentence with a capital letter.

1. The street was dark. _____ had no lights.

2. Brianna is happy. _____ found her kitten.

3. Jared likes to run. _____ can run fast.

4. My dad works hard. _____ builds houses.

5. Mrs. White came to see us. _____ is our friend.

6. This animal is not a cow. _____ is a goat.

Word Usage—Pronouns

Using They, We

The word **they** can take the place of a word that names more than one person, animal, or thing.

The wagons were big.
They went west.

The word **we** can take the place of the names of more than one person. **We** includes the speaker.

My brothers and I have fun.
We like to laugh.

Put a (circle) around **they** or **we** to show which word can take the place of the underlined words.

1. The balloons went up.
   (They)   We

2. My friends and I go to school.
   They   We

3. These shoes are wet.
   They   We

4. My dad and I live in a new house.
   They   We

5. Joel and I ran to the barn.
   They   We

Word Usage—Pronouns

Writing Sentences

Write a sentence to go with each of these sentences. Use **he, she,** or **it.**

An apple is round.

My brother is tall.

Write three sentences about something you and your friends like to do. Use **I** in the first sentence. Use **we** or **they** in your other sentences.

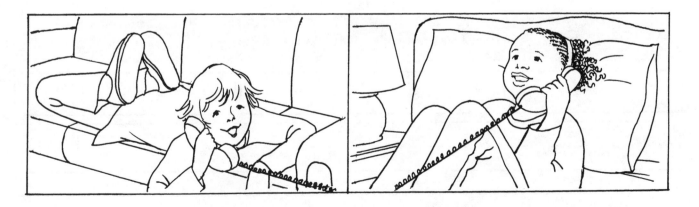

Sentence Building—Writing Sentences

Words and Sentences

Put a (circle) around each word that is made from two words.
Draw a line to show where the words are joined.

doghouse   happen   blanket   raincoat

kitten   horseshoe   cowboy   rabbit

Put a (circle) around **a** or **an** before each word below.

a

an   airplane

a

an   girl

a

an   ear

a

an   dress

Put a (circle) around the right word to complete each sentence.
Cross out the group of words that is not a sentence.

He

1. Reba is kind. She is a nice girl.

It

We

2. Nick and I played ball. It   had fun.

We

3. Two hats in the store window. They   were brown.

Write two sentences about your family. Use some of the words in the box.

| a | he | she | I | we | they | an |

A Story

A story should make sense.
The sentences must be in the right order.

The pictures tell a story in the right order.
Number the sentences to match the pictures.

_____ The ball came fast.

_____ Sidney got a home run.

_____ Sidney was ready to bat.

_____ He hit the ball hard.

A Story

A story must be in the right order.

It was good to eat.

Travis got a fish.

He cooked it in a pan.

1. _____

2. _____

3. _____

Writing a Story

Write four sentences that tell a story about something you did in school today. Remember to put your sentences in the right order.

1. _____

2. _____

3. _____

4. _____

83

A Story

A story should make sense.
The sentences must tell about only one thing.

Draw a line through the sentence that does not belong in each story.

Lan and Arif are making a boat.
They are working hard.
Lan has a bike.
Their boat will be small.

LaTisha has the flu.
She must stay in bed.
Her shoes are red.
She cannot go to school.

The street is busy.
My dad works at a store.
Many cars and trucks go by.
They stop when the light is red.

A Story

A story must tell about only one thing at a time.

Jin told two stories, but he mixed them up.
Find the sentences that tell a story about each picture.
Write the numbers of the sentences under the pictures.

1 _____

_____

_____

2 _____

_____

_____

1. I was on the airplane.

2. Many cars were in the race.

3. The airplane took off.

4. I liked flying.

5. One car got a flat tire.

6. The other cars did not stop.

85

Writing a Story

The sentences in a story must tell about only one thing at a time.

Draw a line through the two sentences that do not tell about these pictures.
Use the three sentences that tell about the pictures to write a story in the
space below.

  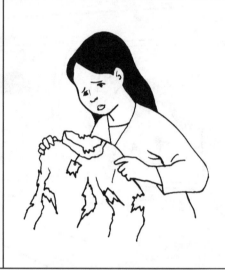

Veda got a new sweater.

My feet are cold.

Her dog took it.

Your hat is funny.

Now it is torn.

_____

- -

_____

- -

_____

- -

_____

A Letter

May 2, 2003

Dear Lee,

   Thank you for the book about horses. It was fun to read.

Your friend,
Zane

Marta forgot to use capital letters in her letter.
Cross out each letter that should be a capital.
Write the capital letter above it.
Use the letter above to help you.

M
march 17, 2003

dear carlos,

   thank you for the rabbit you gave me. i will take good care of it.

your friend,
marta

A Letter

Put a (circle) around each comma.

June 8, 2003

Dear Grandma,

Thank you for the box of paints.
I will make a picture for you.

Love,
Su Ling

Keenan forgot to use commas in his letter.
Put the commas in for him.
Use the letter above to help you.

July 4 2003

Dear Uncle Don

Thank you for taking us on a
picnic. We all had a good time.

Love
Keenan

Writing a Letter

Write a letter to a friend. Start with the date.
Put capital letters and commas at the right places.

89

Story and Letter Writing

Draw a line through the sentence that does not tell about the pictures.
Number the other sentences in the right order to tell a story about the pictures.

_____ This is an old truck.

_____ She sat in the back.

_____ The bus stopped.

_____ Emily got on.

Cross out each letter that should be a capital letter.
Write the capital letter above it.
Put commas where they belong.

november 24 2003

dear owen

thank you for the yellow bird. i got a cage for it.

your friend

kira

Check Up: Sentences

Today is April 25 2003.

There s a game at 3:00.

We ll play ball at the park.

Dara where s my glove?

It s on the top shelf.

Thank you Dara.

Cross out each letter that should be a capital, and write the capital letter above it. Put periods, question marks, and exclamation marks where they should go.

1. our game is on friday, april 25

2. mr c j price is our coach

3. who hit that ball

4. what a great catch

Write sentence 1 here. Use abbreviations for the day and month.

_____

- - - - - - - - - - - - - - - - - - - -

_____

91

Check Up: Writing

Rashid forgot to use capital letters and commas in his letter. Write the letter the right way on the lines below.

october 10 2003

dear shawna

    thank you for asking me to come to your party. i'll see you on friday!

        your friend
        rashid